*To my parents,*
*for their endless love and sacrifices.*

*And to my beloved,*
*for being my peace, strength, and inspiration.*

# BREATHE.
# IT'S OKAY TO PAUSE

## A GUIDE TO SLOWING DOWN AND FINDING PEACE IN A RUSHING WORLD

MRIGANKA DAS

Made with ❤ on the Notion Press Platform
www.notionpress.com

# Contents

# About The Author

*Mriganka Das is a B.Com graduate from Gauhati Commerce College and a national-level archery player. With a deep passion for self-growth, mindfulness, and emotional well-being, The author uses his words to guide young minds toward peace in a world full of noise and pressure.*

*Through his journey as a student, athlete, and observer of life, he has experienced both the weight of expectations and the quiet strength of pausing. His writing reflects a blend of discipline from sports, insight from academics, and empathy from lived experience.*

*In his debut book, "Breathe. It's Okay to Pause", Mriganka encourages readers- to slow down, reconnect with themselves, and realize that true success includes inner calm.*

*This book is not just his story, but a heartfelt offering for anyone caught in the rush, reminding them that rest is powerful, and peace is a purpose.*

# PREFACE

In today's fast-paced world, the pressure to always be doing more can feel overwhelming. Every notification, deadline and comparison makes us believe that we must hustle nonstop. But what if the key to success and happiness lies not in doing everything all at once, but in knowing when to pause?

This book is an invitation to breath, to slow down, and to recognize that **not everything is to be done today.** Through reflection, practical advice, and simple exercises, you will learn how peace can be your greatest achievements.

# Acknowledgements

Writing this book has been a journey of learning, growth, and healing—one I could not have taken alone.

I am deeply grateful to my family and my beloved, whose patience, love, and encouragement gave me the strength to pause when I needed it most and keep going when the path felt uncertain.

Thank you to everyone who listened with an open heart, believed in this message, and inspired me to share it with the world.

And to you, dear reader—thank you for taking this moment to breathe with me. May this book bring you comfort, hope, and the gentle reminder that it's okay to pause.

From the bottom of my heart, thank you.

# I
# When Everything Feels Urgent

The world around us move fast- faster than ever before. Phones beep with messages, deadlines approach relentlessly, and everywhere you look, people seem to be sprinting towards the next big thing. It's easy to feel overwhelmed, pressured and anxious, as if you must act on every notification and complete task immediately.

But is every task truly urgent? Often, the felling of urgency is a trick of the mind- a conditioned reaction to external pressures.

Recognize this: your mind and body need rest. Rushing without reflection leads to mistakes and burnout. The truth is that, the human mind and body are not made to operate in constant high gear. Without pause, your energy drains, creativity stalls, and decision become impulsive rather than thoughtful. Constant urgency leads to burnout and burnout keeps you from reaching your true potential.

Think about a time when you rushed through something important- perhaps a test, a conversation or a creative project. How did it turn out? Chances are the results were not your best. When you allow yourself to breath, to slow down, and to consider what truly needs your attention, you perform better, think clearer, and fell more in control.

So the next time you feel overwhelmed by the "must do" list, pause and ask: Does this need to be done now? Will doing this right now bring me closer to my goals or just distract me?

By learning to say no to the unnecessary urgencies, you feel yourself to say yes to what really matters. And when you do that, you will find peace even in a busy world.

Remember: urgency is often a feeling, not a fact. You have the power to choose your pace

# II

# The Cost of Constant Hustle

In a world that never pauses, hustling has become more than a work ethic—it has turned into an identity. We wear our busyness like a badge of honour. "I've been swamped," we say, almost proudly. But what is the real cost of this endless chase?

### The Illusion of Productivity

The hustle culture glorifies overworking, as if working 16 hours a day is the only path to success. We're told that sleep is for the weak, and breaks are for the lazy. But in chasing this mirage of nonstop productivity, we begin to blur the line between being busy and being effective.

Think about it: how often do we equate movement with progress? Just because your calendar is full doesn't mean you're moving closer to your dreams. Sometimes, the person doing the most is actually getting the least meaningful work done.

### Burnout Isn't a Badge

Burnout is real, and it's not a weakness—it's a warning. Your body will eventually revolt against the chaos you force it into. Headaches, anxiety, irritability, fatigue—these are not random events; they are signs.

We weren't designed to be machines. Even machines need cooling time. Your mind and body require rest, reflection, and restoration. Without these, your motivation withers, creativity dies, and joy becomes a distant memory.

Real strength lies not in how much you can endure, but in how well you can sustain your purpose over the long term.

### The Neglected Relationships

In the hustle, relationships often take the back seat. We cancel dinners, ignore phone calls, and delay vacations. We believe we'll make time for them "once we succeed." But life doesn't wait for your achievements. Your parents grow older; your siblings move on, your friends drift away.

Regret is a cruel companion. Don't let ambition cost you connection. Because at the end of the day, it's not your awards but your relationships that will sit beside you in life's quietest moments.

### Peace Is Also a Form of Progress

It's easy to believe that stillness equals stagnation. But silence can be incredibly powerful. Some of the greatest breakthroughs happen in the quiet moments—when we walk alone, breathe deeply, or simply pause.

Hustling without direction is like running on a treadmill—you're moving fast but going nowhere. It's in moments of reflection that we realign, reset, and redirect ourselves toward what truly matters.

Don't be afraid to slow down. Don't fear a blank day in your planner. Sometimes, pausing is the most productive thing you can do.

The Courage to Redefine Success

For too long, success has been measured in numbers—grades, salaries, followers, achievements. But what if success was redefined as peace of mind, freedom of time, and depth of relationships?

Choosing balance doesn't mean you're less ambitious. It means you're brave enough to live on your terms. To hustle wisely, not blindly.

Success without mental health is hollow. Money without meaning is misery. Hustle, yes—but not at the cost of your health, your heart, or your happiness.

Consider the story of Sophia, a bright young professional who landed her dream job at 24. She worked tirelessly—12-hour shifts, skipping meals, cutting off friends. She climbed the ladder fast. But by 27, she was diagnosed with anxiety and chronic fatigue. One day, she quit it all. And then she runs a small business on her terms, earns less but smiles more. Her definition of success changed, and so did her life.

Not everyone needs to crash to reset. Learn from stories like Sophia before life forces you to.

**Final Reflection**

The cost of constant hustle is far greater than we realize—until it's too late. In trying to be everything, we forget to just be. So, pause. Breathe. Rethink your pace. You're not behind. You're not missing out. Life is not a race—it's a journey. And you have every right to dance to your own beat.

# III

# Disconnect to Reconnect

In a world where being online is almost synonymous with being alive, we've forgotten what it means to truly live.

We wake up and the first thing we do is reach for our phones. A hundred notifications, endless scrolling and within five minutes of opening our eyes, we are already connected- to everyone and everything except ourselves. Our minds are crammed with voices, opinions, judgements, and filtered snapshots of people's in social media's highlighted reels. We're most plugged in than ever, yet more distant from our own thoughts, values and peace.

It wasn't always this way, think back to your childhood- maybe you woke up and stared out the window for a while. You played outside with friends, not with virtual avatars. You took long walks without the urge to share it online. That slow, raw, connected life might seem outdated now- but it was real. And most of us are silently craving a return to those quiet nostalgic memories.

### The Illusion of Connection

Modern life makes us believe we're constantly connected- but what we're really experiencing is stimulation, not connection. You might have 5000 followers, but how many of them know the fear that keeps you awake at night? How many would sit beside you in silence when you're struggling?

Arjun, a college student told his friend something that stuck: "I posted everything, but I feel like nobody knows me". It was when he took a voluntary one- month break from social media that he started rediscovering himself. He read alone and reconnected with his sister after years, "That month gave me back my peaceful mind," he said.

It's not about deleting apps or becoming a monk, it's about balance: about knowing that your attention is sacred, so invest it in yourselves.

### Why We Fear Silence

Have you ever tried sitting alone without a screen? Even for few hours?

At first it feels uncomfortable. Thoughts rush in, regrets surface, question arises and we immediately try to escape by opening social media, sending message, playing music. But here's the truth: most people fear silence because it introduces them to themselves. And sometimes, meeting yourself could be the hardest thing. But silence is where healing starts.

When you disconnect from world-even briefly, you reconnect with your emotions, your values and your dream. You realize that you're not just a consumer of content, but a creator of your life. You stop reacting and start reflecting. You realize that inner peace was never lost; it was just buried under noise.

### Simple Practices to Reconnect

You don't need to move to the mountains to find peace. Start small, Start today.

1. **<u>Solo Morning</u>**: Spend the first 60 minutes after waking up without your phone. Let you first thoughts be yours, not about the world.

**2. <u>Mindful Walk</u>**: Leave your phone at home. Walk slowly; notice the trees, the winds, the sky, the current of the river water, the smell. This is life whispering to you.

3. **<u>Journalising</u>**: Write one page every night, not for likes or followers, but for clarity. Ask yourself: What did I fell today? What did I learn?

4. **<u>Digital Sabbath</u>**: Choose one day a week, maybe the weekend to go offline for the day, no social media, and no virtual games. Use the time to read, walk, write or spend time with your parents.

Over the time, you will find that these small practices create space in your life for something deeper- real connection.

**The Power of Presence**

Disconnection from devices is ultimately a reconnection to presence, to this moment.

Imagine sitting with a friend who is fully present- no phone, no distraction. Every word that they say feels heavy with meanings. Now imagine being that person for yourself, you will find the true meaning of peace and connection within yourself. Disconnecting isn't about being anti-technology, it's about being pro-self. It's about reclaiming your time, your breath, and your stillness.

**You Don't Have to Prove Anything**

The need to be "visible" often drives us. We feel that if we don't post, don't comment, don't react, we will be forgotten. But here's something powerful to remember: *You don't have to prove your existence every day.* Your worth is not measured by views; your presence is not validated by likes. You are enough even when you are silent

In fact, it's your absence that people often feel your real presence, so don't be afraid to go offline. You're just reappearing in the place that matters most.

Silence is no empty, it's full of answers.

Disconnect.

Reconnect with your heart.

With your life.

With what makes you whole.

# IV

# The Myth of FOMO

Have you ever felt like you're being left behind? That while you're just trying to figure things out and everyone else seems to be raced ahead- getting better jobs, buying cars, falling in love, travelling the world?

Those feelings are called- FOMO or Fear of Missing Out.

FOMO is the uncomfortable thought that maybe you're not doing enough, not living your life the way others are. It creeps in quietly when you scroll through social media or hear people talk about their plans. Suddenly, your peaceful routine fells boring, you started feeling that your achievements are small. You start to question yourself.

But let me tell the truth: FOMO is a trick your mind plays on you. It makes you believe you are behind, when in reality, everyone is figuring things out silently, just like you.

### What you see isn't the whole story

In today's world, we see more people's lives than before due to social media and technological upgradation. Social media gives us a front row seat into everyone's highlights- the job offers, vacations, celebrations and perfect pictures of their life.

But remember this:

People only show what they want others to see.

You don't see the nights they cried after failing an exam, the loneliness behind the selfies, or see their worries, struggles or bad days.

So when you feel left behind, ask yourself: *"Am I comparing my full life to someone else's filtered moments?"*

If yes, stop. It's not fair for you.

**Everyone has a Different Timeline**

Think about this:

Some people become successful at 22. Some gets success at 42.

Some find love at 20. Some gets at 35.

Some lose everything and rebuild from scratch.

There is no single path in life. No perfect age to succeed; everyone's journey is different.

If someone else is running ahead, it doesn't mean you've lost the race. Life is not a race. It's a personal journey. And your pace is right pace for you. Sometimes the best things take time to grow.

Imagine you're at a hospital. Everyone is waiting for their name to be called. Some go in quickly, others have to wait. But everyone has a different reason to be there, everyone waiting for different doctor, different problems and a different solution.

Just because someone got called in before you, doesn't mean you've been forgotten. Your time will come too. You're not behind- you're just waiting for your right moment. *Life is the same.*

**How to Beat FOMO and Find peace**

Here are a few simple ways to deal with the Fear of Missing Out (FOMO):

1. **<u>Be Grateful for What You Have</u>**: Look at your surroundings. May be you don't have everything, but you have something. A roof, a gaol, health, hope, stay grateful, Gratitude changes how we see life.
2. **<u>Take Break From Social Media</u>**: When everything you see makes you feel small, step away. Take a break from the screen. Go outside, talk to people, read, write diary. Live your real life, not your online one.
3. **<u>Celebrate Small Wins</u>**: Did you wake up early today? Did you complete your to do list? Did you plant tree? Did you help the beggar? That's a win. Don't ignore it, big success is built on small, daily steps.
4. **<u>Remind Yourself, It's Ok To Go Slow</u>**: You're not a machine. You're a person. It's ok to rest. It's ok to pause. Going slow does not mean you've failed. It means you're taking care of yourself.

FOMO tells you that you're missing out. But what if you're actually living it more deeply than others? Because while other chasing everything, maybe you're learning and enjoying the simple things- your growth, your peace, your dream, your pace. Don't let the noise of the world drown out the value of your own journey.

Breathe.

Slow down.

You're life is not a competition, it's a creation.

And you're just doing fine at your own pace.

# V

# Ask Purpose, Not Pressure

We live in a world that constantly asks us, "What's next?" "What job?" "What degree?" "What milestone?"

But what if the better question was- (why?) "Why are you doing what you're doing?" not everything we do must come from pressure. Something can – and should- come from purpose.

### The Pressure Loop

Many of us are caught in what I call the "pressure loop".

You see someone post their promotion.

You scroll through another start up story

You hear a friend talking about their CAT coaching, UPSC plans, or foreign studies.

You're heartbeat quickens and you start setting goals, not because they're meaningful to you, but because they sound impressive to others. This is how we drift from our real purpose; we begin to live under borrowed expectations.

### The Power of Purpose

Now pause, imagine doing something not because it earns praise- but because it aligns with what you believe in.

This is the difference between pressure and purpose.

*Pressure screams,* "You have to!"

*Purpose whispers,* "You want to."

Pressure leads to burnout; whereas purpose leads to fulfilment.

Let's take an example:

Meet Ananya, she cracked an MBA entrance and joined a reputed B-school, but found herself unhappy, anxious and lost. After a break, she joined a non-profit working with children- and despite the lower salary, she smiles every day, feeling alive.

Her journey wasn't a failure. It was realignment from pressure to purpose.

### *Questions that Matters*

Start asking yourself:

- Am I doing this for myself or with someone else's approval?

- If no one ever praised me, would I still do it?

- What activities make me lose track of time- in a good way?

Purpose is not always big or flashy. It can be as small as helping your parents with their shop, helping friends with their studies, it could be anything that makes you feel full of purpose.

### *Purpose Feels Light, Pressure Feels Heavy*

When you act from purpose:

- You feel calm even when tired.

- You feel clarity even in chaos.

- You feel peace even when you're not progressing at lightning speed.

When you act from pressure

- You feel overwhelmed even while succeeding.

- You feel anxious even while praised

- You feel empty even while achieving.

You are allowed to slow down- not to quit, but to listen to your inner voice.

You are allowed to rethink- not to delay, but to realign.

You are allowed to pause- because that's where purpose often finds you.

Purpose lives in pattern, in your habits, your values, your dreams. Remember: you don't find purpose, you notice it, nurture it, and you live it.

Live is not under pressure, but with purpose. Because at the end of the day, peace is not found in how fast you went- but in whether you went in the right direction.

# VI

# Rest is Not Laziness

We live in a world that worships hustle. A world where people wear exhaustion like a badge of honour and busyness is confused with productivity. Where "doing nothing" is equivalent with being unworthy. But here's the truth the world doesn't say enough: *rest is not laziness, it is survival, repair and is powerful.*

### The Stigma of Rest

From our school days, we were taught that only hard work leads to success- and that any pause, any moment spent not producing something measurable, is a waste. We hear phrases like "don't waste time", or "idle mind is devil's workshop". Eventually, we internalize a dangerous message that, *if I'm not constantly doing, I am failing.*

The thinking has shaped a generation that feels guilty for taking a nap, for saying no to late night grind session, for steeping back from social media commitments or even watching the rain in silence. We feel the need to justify our rest, as if taking care of ourselves is a crime that needs an excuse.

But pause for a moment and ask yourself- What if rest is part of the work?

### *Nature Doesn't Rush- And Yet Everything Gets Done*

Look at the nature. Trees don't grow overnight. The seasons don't compete with each other. A rose doesn't bloom faster because another flower bloomed first. Winter comes and everything slows down- animal hibernate, leaves fall and the earth breath. This is not failure, this is rhythm.

Yet we, as humans, have tried to separate ourselves from the natural rhythm. We work beyond our limits, chase impossible schedules, and feel guilty when we need time to recharge. Even machines shut down for maintenance- so why can't we?

### *Rest Restores*

There's a story of man who went to work with a young seasoned lumberjack. They began chopping trees at dawn. The young man worked without a break, full of energy and ambition. The older lumberjack took regular pauses- for water, for lunch, even just to breath.

At the end of the day, the older man had cut more trees. The young man was surprised and asked, "How did you beat me when I worked continuously?"

The old man smiled and said, "Because while you were chopping continuously, I was also sharpening my axe."

That's what rest does. It sharpens your axe. It resets focus, rebuilds your strength and realigns your purpose.

### *You Deserve Rest Even If....*

*Even if you didn't finish everything on your to do list*

*Even if others are still working*

*Even if you're not felling or burnout*

*You deserve rest simply because you are human.*

### Make Peace with Pause

Here's a practical habit: schedule non-negotiable rest hours in your week. It could be your Sunday afternoon, evening walk without your phone, or just sitting under the sky doing nothing. You'll be surprised how much clarity and calm these small pauses can bring.

Also, learn to say "no" without guilt. The world won't stop rotating if you decline a late-night project or leave a group chat for your mental peace. Your body and mind will thank you.

### Rest Is Resistance

In a culture that constantly shouts "go faster," choosing to rest is an act of rebellion. It's saying "I am not a machine. I am a soul. I need time to feel, heal and just being myself."

So, next time someone says, "Why are you wasting time?"- smile gently and say, "I am resting. I am growing invisible roots."

Because one day, those roots will help you bloom in ways hustle alone never could.

# VII

## Success without Burnout

In today's fast-paced, hyper-competitive world, success is often equated with sleepless nights, packed schedules, and relentless hustle. Somewhere along the way, the idea of thriving got replaced with surviving. But what if I told you that real success doesn't demand you to burn yourself out? What if the highest version of success actually comes with balance, joy, and sustainability?

Burnout isn't a badge of honour—it's a warning sign. And yet, many of us wear it like an achievement. We post about our sleepless hustle, glorify stress, and believe that if we're not constantly exhausted, we're not doing enough.

But success at the cost of health, peace, and relationships isn't success—it's a slow form of self-abandonment.

### The Myth of "Push till You Break"

Growing up, we often hear: "Push harder," "No pain, no gain," or "Sleep is for the weak." These ideas shaped a generation that works overtime not just at jobs, but at life itself. But pushing till you break isn't strength—it's disconnection from your own limits.

Ask yourself: Are you chasing your dreams, or running from burnout?

You were not made to wake up tired every day. You were not made to be a machine. Your life isn't just about output—it's about experience.

### *Redefining Success*

Let's reframe success:

Success isn't just reaching the finish line—it's about how you feel while getting there.

It's about creating, not just completing.

It's about maintaining your mental clarity, physical energy, and emotional connection throughout the journey.

A calm mind can solve problems faster than an overworked one. A rested body can endure more than a drained one. A soul at peace creates deeper, more impactful work than one in chaos.

Look around—those who sustain success over time are not those who burned out the fastest, but those who learned when to pause, when to breathe, and when to reset.

Take the example of Aditi, a young entrepreneur from Assam. At 25, she ran a successful online art business. At first, she followed the "hustle till you make it" mentality. She worked 16-hour days, skipped meals, and even ignored early signs of anxiety. Eventually, she broke down. Doctors told her it was burnout.

During her recovery, she rebuilt her work style. She implemented work-life balance, learned to say no, and focused on quality over quantity. Today, she still runs a successful business—only now, she wakes up joyful, works mindfully, and sleeps peacefully. She didn't give up her dream. She just chose not to sacrifice herself for it.

### Build Systems, Not Stress

To succeed without burnout:

- Create boundaries. Know when to stop.

- Practice rest as part of your productivity, not its enemy.

- Learn to prioritize. Not everything needs your energy.

- Celebrate small wins, not just final goals.

- Find meaning in what you do—not just results.

You don't need to rush to be successful. You need clarity, focus, and compassion—especially for yourself.

### Remember:

You are not lazy for needing rest.

You are not failing for going slow.

You are not behind. You're just moving at your own pace.

Success without burnout is not only possible—it's essential. You can be ambitious and peaceful, driven and mindful, successful and healthy.

Let your success be sustainable, not self-destructive. Because true success isn't just about achieving great things—it's about feeling whole while doing it.

# VIII

# Your Worth Is Not You Working

We live in a society that often measures a person's worth by how much they do-how many hours they put in, how productive their day was, how many achievements they stack by the end of the week. The faster you run, the more you're praised. The more you produce, the more you're seen.

But let me say this clearly and unapologetically:

Your worth is not your working.

You are not a machine. You are not a checklist. You are not the weight of your deadlines.

***You Are Enough - As You Are***

Before your resume was written, before your report cards existed, before anyone could measure your "productivity"-you were already enough. The moment you took your first breath, you were valuable. Not for what you could do, but simply because you are you.

So many people tie their self-esteem to their ability to deliver results. And while being dedicated and goal-oriented is admirable, it's dangerous when your entire identity begins to revolve around performance.

When the question, "How are you?" gets answered with "Busy," it's a sign of a society in need of healing.

You are not meant to earn your existence by grinding endlessly.

You are not "falling behind" because you needed rest today.

You are still worthy- even on your most unproductive days.

The Trap of Constant Productivity

Let's talk about a common scenario.

Imagine Ram, a young professional who wakes up each day to a full calendar. Zoom calls, deadlines, emails. He powers through his to-do list, skipping meals, pushing breaks, postponing joy. Every evening, he checks his screen time and feels proud of hitting 12-hour workdays. He falls asleep exhausted, but validated- because his busyness felt like proof of his value.

But over time, Ram starts to feel empty. Not because he failed, but because his self-worth was entirely built around work. He didn't know who he was outside of being productive. His hobbies faded. His peace eroded. His relationships suffered.

Sound familiar?

This is not just Ram's story. It's the story of a generation raised to believe that doing equals deserving.

### Why This Belief Hurts

It leads to burnout. Constantly pushing without pause can damage your health- mentally and physically.

It causes shame on days when you're less productive, even if rest was what you truly needed.

It discourages joy for the sake of joy. We forget how to do things simply because they make us happy.

It alienates us from our inner self- who we are beyond the labels of jobs, marks, or money.

*Let's reminds yourself:*

You are allowed to be valuable even when you are still.

You are allowed to rest without guilt.

You are allowed to just be.

### ***Finding Worth beyond Work***

Meet Anirban, a software engineer from Guwahati. For years, his identity was tied to being the "best performer" at work. He climbed ranks, won awards, and stayed late to impress bosses. But inside, he was drowning. One day, he took a short break and travelled to Meghalaya for peace. He didn't code. He didn't plan. He just existed.

That short break made him realize something profound:

His joy, his peace, and his identity didn't need to be earned- they were already within him.

He came back and restructured his life. Fewer work hours, more music, journaling, and laughter with friends. His productivity didn't drop. In fact, it became more meaningful- because now it wasn't trying to prove anything.

### **Detaching Self-Worth from Work**

Here's how you can begin:

- *Practice Self-Compassion*: When you take a break, talk to yourself kindly. You're not "lazy." You're human.

- *Find Joy Beyond Output*: What lights you up when no one's watching? Dance, write, draw or run. Do it for you.

- *Celebrate Being, Not Just Doing*: Make time to simply exist. Not every hour needs a result attached.

- *Redefine Success*: Success is not just what you achieve—it's also how peaceful you feel while achieving it.

You were not born to earn approval through exhaustion.

You were born to experience life fully- its silence and sound, its rhythm and pause, its ambition and stillness.

You are more than your grades.

You are more than your job title.

You are more than your productivity.

Let's this chapter be your permission slip- to rest, to slow down, to detach your velocity. Your existence is not a project to complete. It's a story to live.

# IX

# Joy in Simple Things

In our rush for success, achievement, and external validation, we often overlook the beauty of the small things-those quiet, fleeting, and seemingly insignificant moments that have the power to heal us, ground us, and fill us with a kind of joy that doesn't need to be chased.

Joy isn't always found in the grand; sometimes it lives in the gentle.

Do you remember those evenings of your childhood when a cup of tea and a slow sunset felt like the most peaceful thing in the world? Or the joy of finding your old comic book collection, dog-eared and dusty, but alive with memories?

That is the magic of simplicity.

***The Illusion of Bigger = Better***

Today's world makes us believe that joy must be bought or earned. It must come with filters, hash tags, and likes. But this illusion keeps us reaching to never resting.

We believe joy is found in exotic travel, high-paying jobs, luxury gadgets, or viral fame. And while those things may excite us momentarily, they rarely nourish us.

True joy, sustainable joy, the kind that lingers in your heart- it often comes in silence, in slowness and in simplicity.

A quiet walk in the garden. Laughing until your stomach hurts. Watching raindrops races on your windowpane. Listening to your grandmother hum an old lullaby.

That's the kind of joy no money can buy. And that's the joy we're forgetting to notice.

### Finding the Beauty in the Ordinary

Let me take you to a little village in Assam, where life moves at a pace slower than most. There's a man named Hari, who runs a small tea stall near the river. Every morning, he wakes up at 5 a.m., sweeps his shop, and makes chai.

He doesn't own a smart phone. He doesn't have any social media. But every customer who walks into his stall leaves with a smile—not just because of the tea, but because of Hari's presence.

He greets everyone by name. He hums while he works. And when you ask him why he's always so cheerful, he says, "there is nothing in continuous hustling, real peace is in stillness. Happiness is a game of small, small things."

That's wisdom wrapped in simplicity.

### Nostalgia: A Path to Rediscover Joy

Let's take a moment to reflect on the past—not to dwell, but to reconnect.

- Do you remember the sound of chalk on blackboards?

- Or the smell of rain on dry soil when school got cancelled?

- Or the joy of riding a cycle for the first time without falling?

These weren't 'milestones' in the traditional sense, but they were the building blocks of a joyful heart. We didn't need much- just curiosity, a little freedom, and someone to share it with.

The reason nostalgia feels so warm is because those were the moments we were fully present. And remember that being present, is the root of all joy.

### How to Cultivate Joy in Simplicity

- *Slow Down*: You can't experience the beauty of the small if you're always racing. Take intentional pauses. Let the moment breathe.

- *Notice Details*: The swirl in your coffee. The wind in your hair. The flicker of sunlight through leaves. These are poems written by the universe.

- *Practice Gratitude*: Keep a journal. Each night, write down 3 simple things that made you smile. A bird's song. A stranger's kindness. Your own actions.

- *Unplug Often*: Step away from screens and into reality. Digital joy fades. Real joy roots you.

- *Celebrate the Mundane*: Make your bed and admire it. Cook a meal and eat it slowly. Call a friend just to hear their voice. These things matter.

### *The Deeper Meaning*

Finding joy in simple things is an act of rebellion in a world that tells you to want more. It saying: "I don't need to chase happiness- I choose to see it, here, now."

It's an acknowledgment that life, in its purest form, is already beautiful.

It's reclaiming peace, bit by bit, from the chaos.

It's learning that you don't need to 'earn' rest, love, or joy. They are your birthright.

Sit by a window tonight. Feel the wind on your face. Drink something warm. Let the world slow down around you.

Ask yourself: What simple thing today made my heart smile?

And then, smile again, because in that moment, you found it.

Joy, in its truest form, is already with you. You just need to look closer.

# X

# The Art of Being Present

In the rush of modern life, we often live everywhere. Our minds leap into future deadlines or past regrets, rarely touching the present moment with full awareness. But the real, vibrant, meaningful life - is only ever available in the now. This chapter is an invitation to return to the present, to breathe deeply into the moment you're in, and to rediscover the joy, peace, and power that come from truly being present.

### What Does It Mean to Be Present?

Being present means immersing yourself fully in what you're doing, feeling, and experiencing - without distraction, judgment, or anticipation. It means drinking your tea and just drinking your tea - not scrolling your phone, not mentally rehearsing a conversation, not stressing about tomorrow's to-do list. It means listening to someone not just to respond, but to understand. It means walking outside and actually seeing the trees, feeling the wind, hearing the birds.

Being present is not about perfect concentration or always being calm. It's about showing up - for your moments, your relationships, and your life. And it is one of the most powerful antidotes to the stress, burnout, and disconnection that plague our generation.

### The Cost of Living Elsewhere

Most people are physically present but mentally absent. We multitask during conversations. We eat while working. We relax with watching TV while texting five different people. And yet, we wonder why our relationships feel shallow, why joy seems fleeting, and why peace never arrives.

This constant mental fragmentation comes at a cost:

- *We miss out on joy:* Simple moments like laughing with friends, the warmth of the sun, or the taste of our food slip away unnoticed.

- *We increase anxiety:* Worrying about the future or replaying the past drains our emotional reserves.

- *We damage our relationships:* Half-presence is no presence at all. People can feel when we're not really with them.

- *We feel unfulfilled:* Even achievements lose their shine when we're never really there to enjoy them.

Living in the past brings regret. Living in the future brings anxiety. Living in the present brings peace.

### The Science of Presence

Modern psychology supports what ancient traditions have long taught: being present improves mental well-being. Mindfulness studies show it reduces stress, enhances memory, and increases happiness. In fact, a Harvard study found that people are happier when their minds are in the present, regardless of what they're doing.

Neuroscientists explain that mindfulness (another word for presence) activates the prefrontal cortex - the brain's centre for decision-making, empathy, and awareness - while reducing activity in the amygdala, the stress centre. Being present literally rewires your brain for calm and clarity.

### Barriers to Being Present

Despite the benefit, staying present isn't easy. Here's why:

- *Overstimulation*: Our phones, notifications, and endless digital feeds constantly pull us away from the now.

- *Fear of Missing Out (FOMO)*: We fear that if we're not multitasking or "in the loop," we'll fall behind.

- *Emotional avoidance*: Being present sometimes means facing uncomfortable feelings - sadness, boredom, loneliness - which we'd rather escape.

- *Conditioned busyness*: We've been taught that doing is more valuable than being. Presence feels unproductive, even when it's deeply healing.

### Small Steps to Presence

You don't need to become a monk or meditate for hours to practice presence. Start small:

- *Single-task*: Do one thing at a time. When you eat, just eat. When you walk, just walk avoid multitasking.

- *Breathe intentionally*: Take 3 deep breaths throughout your day and bring awareness to how your body feels.

- *Put the phone away*: Especially during meals or conversations. Give your full attention.

- *Use sensory grounding*: Notice 5 things you can see, 4 you can touch, 3 you can hear, 2 you can smell, and 1 you can taste. It's a powerful technique of meditation too.

- *Daily "pause time"*: Schedule 10-15 minutes daily to do nothing - sit, breathe, and be calm.

### Presence in Relationships

How often do we listen to reply rather than to understand? Presence is the most powerful gift we can give in relationships.

Be there fully - look into their eyes, really hear their words, and hold space for their emotions. You'll find that even difficult conversations become easier when you're not distracted by inner chatter.

Presence builds trust. It deepens connection. And it says, "You matter."

### Presence in Work and Study

Being present doesn't mean being slow. It means being focused. Athletes call it "the zone," artists call it "flow," and monks call it "mindfulness." In that state, productivity soars and creativity flows.

Whether you're writing an exam, preparing a report, or practicing archery (like I do!) - The best of your work comes when you're immersed in the moment. Try working in distraction-free blocks. You'll finish more in less time, and with less stress.

### *Presence in Pain*

One of the hardest places to be present is in discomfort. But presence in pain can be transformative.

When sadness arises, instead of distracting yourself, try sitting with it. Name the feeling. Breathe into it. It will move through you faster and with less suffering than resistance ever could.

### *Presence Is Power*

Being present is not passive. It's a bold choice in a world that constantly demands your attention. It's saying:

I will not rush through my life.

I will not let fear and distraction steal my peace.

I will live this moment, fully - because it is the only one I truly have.

Presence reconnects you with yourself. It reminds you of your aliveness. It helps you hear your inner voice. It grounds you when the world feels chaotic.

Close your eyes for a moment. Breathe in slowly. Exhale gently. Now ask yourself:

"Where am I, really?"

Are you in your head, chasing a future that hasn't arrived? Are you stuck in a past you can't change? Or are you here, now, alive in this breath, in this body, in this beautiful moment?

The art of being present is the art of being alive.

So, promise yourself that, "Tomorrow morning, before I touch my phone, I will sit up, breathe in deeply, and just be. Feel the breath. Listen to the sounds around. Welcome the day with presence."

That's where your peace lives.

# XI
# Redefining Productivity

"You are not a machine. You are not measured by your output alone. Redefine what it means to truly be productive- in work, in joy, in being human."

We live in a world obsessed with doing. A world where productivity is worn like a badge of honour, where rest is shamed, and where being busy is confused with being successful. Every day, from social media to motivational videos, we are told: hustle harder, grind longer; do not stop until you're proud. But amidst all this noise, one crucial truth is forgotten - we are human beings, not human doings.

### What Is Productivity, Really?

The word "productivity" originally meant the rate at which goods are produced. It belonged to factories and machines - systems designed for maximum output. Somehow, over time, we applied that same logic to human lives. We started treating people like machines, measuring our worth by how much we get done in a day.

But let me ask you this:

- Are you productive when you send 50 emails and end the day feeling empty?

- Are you unproductive if you spent the day reconnecting with your passion, with your loved ones, and with your peace?

Modern productivity needs a new definition — one that includes fulfils, balance, intention, and health. Productivity is not just about doing more; it's about doing what matters.

### The Lie of Constant Output

From school to the workplace, we're taught that more is better. More grades. More goals. More hours. More hustle. But here's the truth: Constant output is not sustainable. It doesn't lead to better results; it leads to burnout, exhaustion, and losing touch with who we are.

Productivity without purpose is just motion without meaning.

Consider Neha, a 25-year-old software developer. She woke up at 6 AM, ran five miles, coded for 10 hours, responded to emails until midnight — and still felt she "hadn't done enough." Why? Because her inner worth was tied completely to her output. No matter what she achieved, it didn't feel like enough. It's a trap many of us fall into.

### Why We Chase Hyper-Productivity

- *External Validation*: We're praised for being busy. It makes us feel important, needed, accomplished - even if internally, we're falling apart.

- *Fear of Falling Behind*: Social media shows us everyone's highlight reels. Someone is always achieving more, earning more or building more. The fear pushes us to overwork.

- *Identity Crisis*: We confuse who we are with what we do. So we keep doing, to feel like we are someone.

- *Guilt of Pausing*: Rest feels like laziness. Doing "nothing" feels wrong, because we've never been taught to values of stillness.

But here's the radical truth: Rest is not a reward - it's a right. And true productivity includes rest.

**The Burnout Epidemic**

You know what's not productive? Burning out. Reaching your goals only to feel lifeless when you get there. Sacrificing your health, joy, or identity for success isn't success – It is survival.

Burnout doesn't just affect your work. It dulls your creativity. It damages relationships. It makes you forget what used to bring you joy. And often, it takes a crash to realize we've been flying too fast, too long, in the wrong direction.

Let's redefine.

**Redefining Productivity: A New Philosophy**

So what if productivity looked like this:

- Doing things that align with your purpose — not just your planner.

- Creating space for rest and reflection — not just meetings and deadlines.

- Measuring success by meaning and impact — not just numbers.

- Balancing effort with ease — not every hour has to be optimized.

Productivity is no longer about doing more. It's about doing what matters - with presence, with purpose, and without losing yourself.

### The Tree That Grew Slow

There's a story of two trees planted at the same time. One grew fast - tall, visible, and impressive. The other grew slow, quietly strengthening its roots. When the storm came, the tall tree snapped. The slow-growing one stood firm.

In life, we often rush to "grow fast," to achieve early, to shine before we're ready. But real productivity — the kind that sustains — comes from depth, not speed. It comes from growing roots.

So if you're feeling behind, remember: Not all progress is visible. Not all growth is fast. But all meaningful growth is worth the time.

### The Productivity-Peace Balance

It's not about choosing peace instead of productivity. It's about integrating both. In fact, when you work from a place of peace, you're more effective, more creative, and more aligned.

Here's how:

- *Intentional Work*: Choose your 3 most important tasks, and give them your focus - rather than chasing 10 things halfway.

- *Boundaries*: Stop working when the workday ends. Don't glorify being "always on."

- *Creative Rest*: Take breaks that refill your energy - walks, art, music, silence.

- *Celebrate Progress*: You don't need to reach the mountain to pause. Celebrate the small climbs.

### Productivity Is Also Joy

What if painting, gardening, journaling, or laughing with friends was productive? Because it is. These moments may not show up on performance graphs, but they keep your spirit alive. And that matters just as much.

A fulfilled person is far more productive in the long run than a burnt-out one.

So, let your joy count.

### Create Your Own Metrics

You are allowed to define success in your own terms.

Maybe your measure of productivity is:

- Hours spent with loved ones.

- Creative energy expressed.

- Progress in healing or mental clarity.

- Number of days you felt balanced.

That's powerful. That's enough.

You don't need to earn your worth. You are worthy.

### A Gentle Revolution

Imagine a world where productivity includes presence.

Where people celebrate rest as a part of success.
Where students aren't anxious about their worth.
Where professionals aren't burning out for applause.
Where humans are allowed to be human.
That world begins with you.

You can lead a gentle revolution — by showing that a meaningful life is not one packed with tasks, but one rich with purpose, connection, joy, and peace.

# XII
# Comparison Kills Clarity

In an age where we are constantly exposed to filtered glimpses of other people's lives, comparison has become an automatic reflex. Social media has intensified this tendency. We scroll through images of others achieving milestones, travelling the world, winning awards, or simply living a life that appears more beautiful than ours. In this endless scroll, a quiet war brews inside our minds- a war of inadequacy, envy, and self-doubt.

Comparison, when left unchecked, clouds our judgment and distorts our clarity. It makes us question our own path, our worth, and our pace in life. And perhaps most dangerously, it makes us lose touch with who we are and what truly matters to us.

### The Trap of Measurement

From a young age, we are conditioned to compare: grades in school, sports performance, looks, achievements, social status. This conditioning follows us into adulthood.

We begin measuring our behind-the-scenes against someone else's highlight reel. The result? "Dissatisfaction".

Think about this: You were content with your progress until you saw a peer posting about a promotion or launching a start up. Suddenly, your journey seems slow, your achievements small, and your efforts insignificant. But is that really the truth?

No. What you see is one chapter of their story- the polished version. What you don't see is their sleepless nights, failed attempts, insecurities, and sacrifices.

### Clarity Comes from Within

True clarity is not external. It doesn't come from looking around. It comes from looking inward.

When we stop comparing and start reflecting, we allow our true values to emerge. What do you want? What makes you feel alive? What kind of life feels meaningful to you? These are the questions that lead to clarity.

You cannot hear your own voice if it's constantly drowned out by the noise of someone else's story. The more you compare, the more you stray from your own path. And the more you stray, the less fulfilled you'll feel.

### The Mental Toll of Comparison

Constant comparison creates anxiety, reduces self-esteem, and fuels imposter syndrome. It leads to burnout, not from overworking, but from over thinking. The brain becomes a battlefield of "should" and "must" that were never truly yours.

Consider this scenario: A friend buys a new car. You suddenly feel the urge to upgrade yours, even though you were perfectly happy with your vehicle. Or maybe someone you follow travels every month, and you begin questioning the worth of your steady routine life.

This kind of thinking erodes gratitude. And gratitude is essential for mental peace.

### Replacing Comparison with Inspiration

Comparison isn't always negative. When conscious, it can fuel inspiration. Instead of saying, "I'm not enough," say, "This motivates me to grow." Instead of envy, choose curiosity. Ask, "What can I learn?"

But remember: inspiration uplifts; comparison belittles.

Shift your mindset. From envy to admiration. From lack to potential. From judgment to acceptance. From racing to flowing.

Practical Ways to Avoid Comparison

- *Digital Detox*: Unfollow accounts that trigger comparison. Follow those who add real value or inspire without pressure.

- *Practice Gratitude*: Maintain a daily gratitude journal. Focus on what you have, what you've overcome, and what you're capable of.

- *Reflect Weekly*: Take time every week to check in with your goals. Are you doing this for you, or to prove something?

- *Celebrate Small Wins*: Recognize your progress. Success is not always visible to the world, but it must be acknowledged by you.

- *Mindful Consumption*: Limit your screen time. What you consume shapes your thoughts.

- *Talk About It*: Often, we silently suffer under the weight of comparison. Talk to a friend, coach, or therapist. Let the feeling out.

### You Are Enough

You are not behind. You are not late. Life is not a race. It is a journey with a unique timeline. The more you compare, the more you lose sight of your uniqueness.

You were born to walk your own path. Don't let someone else's map distract you from your destination.

Peace comes not from winning the race but from realizing there was never a race to begin with. And that's clarity! It was always within you.

So the next time you're tempted to compare, pause. Breathe. Come back to yourself.

Because comparison kills clarity. But presence? That brings it back.

# XIII

# Gentle Goals, Not Harsh Deadlines

We live in a culture that celebrates speed. "Hustle harder," "No pain, no gain," and "Sleep is for the weak" are glorified mottos in modern life. But beneath this rush hides a dangerous myth: that harsh deadlines and constant urgency are the only paths to achievement. What if, instead, we allowed room for gentleness-setting goals that grow with us rather than crush us?

What if our journey toward growth felt nourishing, not exhausting?

This chapter is a gentle rebellion against burnout. It's an invitation to redefine achievement, not as a race, but as a rhythm. Because you don't have to destroy your peace to build a meaningful life.

### The Problem with Harsh Deadlines

Deadlines are not the enemy. They help us stay accountable. But when deadlines are unrealistic, rigid, or fuelled by fear, they become damaging. They turn progress into punishment and learning into pressure.

How many times have you set a goal like, "I'll finish this entire course in 7 days," or "I'll lose 10kg in a month," only to feel anxious the whole way and disappointed when you fell short? We've been trained to think that if we don't rush, we won't succeed.

But here's the truth: rushing robs you of quality, joy, and self-trust.

Deadlines driven by insecurity don't motivate- they suffocate.

### Gentle Goals: The Alternative

Gentle goals honour the process, not just the outcome. They're rooted in kindness, not fear. Instead of asking, "How fast can I finish this?" gentle goals ask, "How can I grow into this with balance?"

They leave space for:

• Rest days

• Mistakes and detours

• Reflection and redirection

• Celebrating small wins

Gentle goals believe in consistency, not intensity. It's about building a life that's sustainable- not just impressive on paper.

### Productivity ≠ Self-Worth

One of the silent killers of peace is this belief: "I am only valuable if I'm being productive."

We measure days by how many tasks we ticked off, not how we felt while doing them. But you're more than your to-do list.

Imagine this: One day, you read a book, took a walk, called a friend, and did some creative work. You didn't "finish everything," but your heart felt full. Was that day wasted?

Absolutely not. In fact, these are the days that fuel the energy for your bigger goals

***Building Gentle Goals: A Simple Framework***

• *Start with Intention, Not Pressure*

Ask: Why is this goal important to me? What feeling am I chasing—validation or meaning?

• *Break It Down, Gently*

Instead of setting one giant deadline, divide the goal into smaller, kind milestones.

Example:

Instead of "Write a book this month," try "Write 500 words each evening after tea."

• *Schedule Rest as a Ritual*

Burnout doesn't come from working. It comes from working without breathing.

Add "slow time" to your planner: walks, music, naps, or simply doing nothing.

• *Track Progress, Not Perfection*

At the end of the day, journal what you did, not what you didn't.

Learn to say: "I showed up today. That counts."

· *Celebrate the Unseen Wins*

Not every win is visible. Some days, not quitting is the real victory.

Celebrate focus, effort, courage, and self-compassion.

**Motivation That Doesn't Hurt**

Gentle goals create lasting motivation. Because you're not running from fear-you're moving toward love. You don't resent your goals; you feel supported by them.

When your goals are rooted in gentleness:

· You're more consistent.

· You recover faster from setbacks.

· You avoid burnout.

· You enjoy the process more.

Today enjoyment is underrated but it is the soul of sustainable success.

**When the World Rushes, You Pause**

There will be pressure from outside. People may say, "You're being lazy," or "Why are you so slow?" But remember: speed means nothing without direction.

You're not behind. You're aligned.

You're not wasting time. You're walking mindfully.

Gentle doesn't mean weak. It means wise. It means choosing a pace that honours both your vision and your wellbeing.

**Gentle ≠ Passive**

Let's clarify one thing: setting gentle goals does not mean lowering your dreams or ambitions. It means you're respecting your energy. You're playing the long game.

You're still showing up, still working hard- but not punishing yourself along the way.

In fact, the most successful people are often the most self-aware. They know when to push and when to pause. They listen to their body, honour their rhythm, and play by their rules- not the internet.

### Final Reflections

Life is not a productivity contest. You weren't born to compete with timers and alarms.

You were born to create, to explore, to connect, and to grow- in ways that feel natural, nourishing, and authentic.

Set goals. Dream big. But remember:

- If it's costing your peace, it's too expensive.

- If it's draining your soul, it's not aligned.

- If you need to slow down, do it.

You are allowed to move gently- and still reach greatness.

# XIV

# Breathe. It's Okay to Pause

The world tells us to run.

Run towards success. Run towards perfection. Run until you become someone worthy of admiration.

And so, we keep running - without asking why, without questioning where this road is taking us. Our feet blister, our hearts pound, our minds scream — but we keep running. We believe that slowing down is weakness. That resting means laziness. That if we pause, we'll fall behind.

But what if I told you that the pause - that quiet, mindful stillness - is not just okay, but essential? That pausing is not falling behind; it is catching up with your own self.

### The Power of the Pause

Pausing is not the absence of ambition - it is the presence of awareness.

A pause is a sacred breath. It's the moment between the inhale and the exhale. It is where clarity lives - in that space where we're not chasing, not proving, not pretending. We are simply being. We are enough.

In a world where everyone is shouting, the pause lets you listen.

In a world obsessed with outcomes, the pause reminds you of presence.

In a world that rewards the loudest, the busiest, the most productive — the pause honours the quiet, the still, and the real.

Think of a song. Without the pauses between notes, it would be just noise. Your life, too, needs pauses to create harmony.

### What Happens When We Don't Pause?

When we ignore the need to rest, we don't become more productive - we become more exhausted. More irritable. More disconnected. Our creativity fades. Our relationships weaken. Our bodies ache and our minds spiral.

We become machines, ticking boxes and chasing metrics, forgetting we are human beings - not human doings.

There's a reason burnout feels like drowning: it suffocates. And yet, we keep pushing because the world has glamorized exhaustion. We wear sleeplessness like a badge. We say, "I'm so busy" with pride. But at what cost?

### Reflection: Ayesha's Wake-Up Call

Ayesha was a young marketing executive in Mumbai. Energetic, ambitious, and always on the move. Her schedule was a wall of meetings, deadlines, and late-night presentations. Her phone was never off. Her mind never stopped.

Until one day, in a crowded local train, she fainted.

It wasn't a dramatic collapse, but it was enough. Enough for her to realize she hadn't eaten properly in two days. Enough for her to hear the anxiety in her mother's voice.

Enough to notice how tired - deeply, soul-tired, she felt.

That day, Ayesha paused.

She took a week off - not to travel, not to party - but to sit, to sleep, to think. She started journaling, walked in parks, drank water slowly, read books that had been gathering dust. And for the first time in years, she heard her own voice again.

The pause changed everything.

She didn't quit her job. But she did quit the race. She set boundaries. She redefined success. And most importantly, she reclaimed her life.

### Pausing Is a Practice

It's not always easy to pause. The world won't pause with you. Notifications will still come. Deadlines will still exist. People will still expect.

But the pause is a choice. A deliberate act of rebellion against chaos. A gentle refusal to let life rush past you.

Here are small but powerful ways to practice pausing:

- Breathe before you respond.

- Take few minutes of silence each morning.

- Step away from your screen every hour.

- Write down your thoughts without editing.

- Drink your tea without distraction.

- Take a walk without headphones.

These are not luxuries. These are life-savers. Soul-savers.

### You Deserve to Rest

If no one has told you this before, let this chapter do it:

You do not have to earn your rest. You deserve to rest simply because you exist. You are not a machine. Your worth is not tied to your productivity.

You are allowed to stop. You are allowed to breathe. You are allowed to live slowly. You are allowed to be.

And the world won't fall apart if you take a break. In fact, you might begin to see it more clearly.

### The Final Message

As this book comes to a close, I want you to take this with you:

Peace is also a form of success.

You do not need to do more, be more, to prove more what matters. You already matter. Your presence is enough.

So pause. Breathe. Rest. Trust. Heal. Reflect. Dream slowly. Live gently.

Let the world run if it wants to.

You, my dear reader, are allowed to pause.

Because that's where you deserve to be your true self - not in the rush, but in the stillness.

So, therefore breathe, it's okay to pause.

www.ingramcontent.com/pod-product-compliance
Lightning Source LLC
Chambersburg PA
CBHW032022140726
47988CB00017BA/1349